Why bother with Jesus?

D0057921

Other Books by
Michael Green

Baptism
Adult baptism, infant baptism and baptism in the Holy Spirit.

Freed to Serve
A radical reassessment of Christian ministry today in the light of New Testament principles and changing social and church practice.

I Believe in the Holy Spirit
The teaching of Scripture and the ministry of the Holy Spirit. A seminal work, revised and updated.

I Believe in Satan's Downfall
A fresh look at the biblical account of evil and the promise of Christ's victory.

Matthew for Today
A lively, penetrating commentary on the Gospel of Matthew, examining the person and teaching of Jesus.

New Life, New Lifestyle
A practical handbook, pointing the way forward for the new Christian.

The Empty Cross of Jesus
An examination of the crucifixion and resurrection of Jesus: the central mysteries of the Christian faith.

You Must be Joking
Popular excuses for avoiding Jesus and his claims.

Why bother with Jesus?

by

MICHAEL GREEN

HODDER AND STOUGHTON
LONDON SYDNEY AUCKLAND TORONTO

British Library Cataloguing in Publication Data

Green, Michael b. 1930
  Why bother with Jesus? – (Hodder Christian paperbacks).
  1. Christian life
  I. Title
  248BV4501.2

ISBN 0 340 24008 3

First published 1979
Ninth impression 1988

Copyright © 1979 by Michael Green.

For those
who do not read
religious books

Contents

I

Why bother?

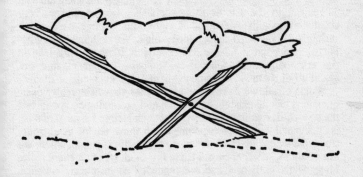

"WHY BOTHER?" is a disease. It is a widespread disease among developed nations. Nothing much seems to matter any more so long as we have our annual rise in wages, so long as the cost of beer and cigarettes is not too high, and so long as we have a colour telly. If you are O.K. on those vital things, why bother about anything else?

The disease has very obviously overtaken Western industrial life. We are not known throughout the world markets for quality products. We don't bother enough. One by one the skilled

crafts have been dying out: inevitably, in some ways, as the
production lines have taken over. But the pride in work has
gone too, and that is neither necessary nor good.

It has affected family life too, this "Why bother?" disease.
Time was when the family would sit round and talk, play
games and make their own amusement. But with three channels
on the T.V., what's the point? Politicians talk about increased
standards of living, but the quality of life in the home has gone
down a lot in recent years. Parents find it easier to give their
children expensive toys rather than their time and interest. It is
too much trouble. And the number of divorces and of mal-
adjusted kids increases all the time – and we wonder why.

It has affected the sporting world, too. Far fewer Europeans
take as active a part in sport as they did ten years ago, and far
more watch sport on the "box". We have become nations of
spectators. It is easier and more exciting that way.

The disease has even taken hold on our concern for the truth.
We aren't that concerned any more. If telling the truth is incon-
venient, almost everybody thinks a "white lie" is acceptable. If
finding the truth is difficult, most of us go for the easy answer,
as set out in the ads or the papers. We no longer feel very
comfortable with questions of right and wrong: we'd much
rather settle for what most people think. We no longer ask what
is true and what is false in different religions: they all lead in
the same direction, don't they? So why bother to find out
about all of them . . . or some of them . . . or even one of them?

Worst of all, we have ceased to bother about the really basic
questions of our existence. Science and technology have solved
the day-to-day problems of living, at any rate so far as hardware
is concerned – relationships are much more tricky. And questions like where we came from, what our life is worth, where we
are going to, whether or not there is a God, whether there is life
after death – all of these are regarded as impractical topics,
which the man of the world can cheerfully leave on one side.
After all, we have got to get on with living. Why bother with
questions like that?

Yes, the disease is widespread in the Western world and it
has bitten deep. Does it matter? I am afraid it does. When a
country is no longer interested in excellence, then it is in real
trouble. When it grows less than vigilant about truth, it
becomes a sitting duck for misleading propaganda. When the
prevailing mood of a nation is that of spectator rather than
participant, it is unlikely to have much say in the conduct of

JIM HUME

Talk politics

politicians
and talks'

port from both religious communities, said he participated in the talks.

The BBC said in addition to Mawhinney and Robinson, the other two politicians who worked out the agreement in West Germany were Jack Allen, chairman of the Official Unionists, the largest Protestant party; and Austin Currie of the moderate Social Democratic and Labor party, the largest Roman Catholic political group.

world affairs. When matters of right and wrong are settled by head-count rather than principle, a moral collapse could well be in the offing. When a people ceases to ask the ultimate questions about life and death, but brushes them under the carpet as unimportant, large scale neurosis is on the way. And when a country suffers from an emptiness of belief and purpose, its future is bleak indeed. The "couldn't care less" attitude is not one to be proud of. "Why bother?" is not a question you find being asked in up-and-coming societies. It is a sign of degeneracy. It is a mark of disease.

2

Why bother with Jesus?

I WAS STANDING at the church door, and one of the church workers came and asked me what book they could give to someone they had in tow who was saying "I believe in God all right, but why bother with Jesus?" I didn't have an immediate answer – which is really, I suppose, why this little book got written. But I realised that the question was an important one, and not merely an expression of the "Why bother?" disease.

A few years ago it would have been the other way round. In the sixties all the clever-clever people were boasting of the death of God and up-to-dateness of Jesus, the Man for Others. But all that has changed. The materialistic values of the sixties have not exactly been repudiated (we are just as keen on our creature comforts and luxuries) but they have been seen to be inadquate. God has come in again with a bang. Not necessarily the traditional understanding of God, whatever that was, but the supernatural in some shape or form. Just a few years ago Billy Graham published a book (not his best book by a long chalk) called *Angels*. If he had done that in the sixties it would have fallen flat on its face. As it was, it sold over a million copies in hardback! It hit the current concern with the supernatural. Witches and black magic have never had it so good. Islam is taking over much of London. Hinduism has never had such an influence as it has today, through transcendental meditation and a multitude of colourful gurus. And new religions are mushrooming all over the place. It's not just the Jehovah's Witnesses and the Mormons that come round to your door nowadays: the Hari Krishna crowd may be dancing in the town square, or the Moonies selling literature outside a supermarket. And if you take the UFO addicts and the horoscope readers into account as well, it is plain that we are not merely religious: we are positively hooked on the supernatural. Materialism is out. It doesn't satisfy and it leaves too much unexplained. The gods have come back with a vengeance.

But why, amid the welter of religions and superstitions which have flooded the market, should we take any notice of Jesus Christ? After all, he has had it all his own way for two thousand years. And, with all due respect to the founder of Christianity, his followers have not made a very impressive or attractive job of commending him to those who are not his fans. So long as some god or other fills the vacuum people have inside, why bother with Jesus?

The whole of this book is an answer to that very important question. But there is a preliminary answer to anyone who is wondering where to turn among the world's religions and the multitude of new cults – or even the occult.

A faith to live by has got to be true. If you go for a lovely fairy tale it will not support you in the hour of death. You will not be able to live it and teach it with conviction. Deep down inside, you know very well that it will not satisfy you unless it is true. It is well known that religions like Mormonism, Jehovah's Witnesses, and Christian Science do not pass that test. Fraud and deceit were around at their birth. However friendly their practitioners, however comfortable their teachings, they do not meet the basic requirement of truth. Jesus does. He is not merely true: he is Truth.

A faith to live by has got to be relevant. It may be true, but if it does not make any difference to ordinary life you can keep it, so far as I am concerned. A lot of what passes for Christianity does not make any noticeable difference to the Sunday congregation. People seem no happier, no kinder, no more honest or easy to live with than those who don't go to church. If church on Sundays is al lthat there is in Christianity, I quite agree with you; why bother with Jesus?

A faith to live by has got to be able to change lives. If it can't remove fear, especially the fear of death; if it can't break habits that have become engrained; if it can't cleanse the conscience from guilt – then it is not what I need. You too, I guess. The glory of Jesus lies in this: nobody has ever been too bad for him to take on, and nobody who ever got into personal touch with Jesus remained unchanged.

A faith to live by has got to offer hope for society at large. If a faith is merely individual, it is petty. If it is merely social, it is ineffective. Part of the wonder of the Christian faith is that it has nerved reform, education, medication, idealism in whole nations, as well as transforming individuals. Unlike Communism it offers the hope of a fulfilment in which all subjects of Jesus will have their share, not merely those who happen to be alive at the end. Unlike Buddhism, which offers us a future with individuality rubbed out (as we will all be absorbed into the One), Jesus promises his people that they will be for ever in his Father's house. Every individual will be there. Everyone will matter. And love, not oblivion, will be the order of the day.

A faith to live by has to appeal to all men. If it is true at all, it must be true for all. Islam is primarily for Arabs and areas they have conquered. Buddhism and Hinduism appeal for the most part to the Eastern temperament. Communism appeals to the oppressed. Zen appeals to the overworked. But Jesus is the man for all races, and for all seasons. Rich and poor, Eskimo and Nubian, educated and savage: the sheer universality of the gospel is just what you would expect if it is the truth of God.

These are some of the things I would look for in a faith that will bear my weight through life and in the face of death. It must be true, relevant, able to change the lives of men and whole societies; it must meet the deepest needs of man, and it must be applicable with equal appeal to all men everywhere. Try that for size with the Moonies, or the J.W.s, and you'll see why I am an enthusiast for Jesus of Nazareth. None but he can meet all those conditions of a faith to live by. That's why it is worth bothering with Jesus.

But I can't (and don't) expect you to take my word for it. Let us look a little deeper, and I hope to show you a good many reasons, in the short chapters which follow, for bothering about Jesus.

3

Bother because he is real

FOR A GREAT many people Jesus is not real. He is make-believe, like Cinderella. He is a folk-lore hero like Jack and the Beanstalk. Most people learn almost nothing about him in home or school these days, and their ideas of Jesus go back to a few occasions in Sunday School to which they were packed off, protesting, while Mum and Dad read the paper in bed. Why should they bother about Jesus?

You try asking a mountaineer one day why he bothers to climb Snowdon – or Everest. He will probably reply "Well, because it is *there!*" That is one very good reason why you should bother with Jesus. He is there. He was a real historical person, and not a myth, a legend or a make-believe hero.

The existence of the Church shows that Jesus is real. Whatever you may think about it, you can't ignore a body of some eight hundred million spread all over the world who can trace their faith back to a historical figure, Jesus of Nazareth. The first Christians were all Jewish, and their religion sprang from the religion of Israel. The only basic difference was this. The Christians were sure that the great Deliverer for whom Judaism was waiting had actually come in Jesus of Nazareth. Round about the year A.D. 30 this new movement called Christianity came out of Judaism with nothing distinctive about it but the radiant conviction that the Deliverer had come. He had died on a cross and thereby in some strange way dealt with human badness and selfishness. He had come alive again: people could get to know him. And he was building a new society, the Christian Church.

This movement spread fast. Within thirty years there were Christians in all the main cities of the Empire, and a rum lot they seemed. A mixture of Jews and Greeks, they did not seem to contain anybody much of influence and importance, and yet they grew. They seemed very happy, very unselfish, very sure they were forgiven men, very full of love to other people. This really was odd. Probably the "love" was a bit warped: after all they called each other "brother" and "sister", and they were reputed to eat somebody's body and blood. Highly suspicious. So they were just the sort of folk on whom Nero could pin the blame for the Great Fire of Rome which he probably started himself in A.D. 64 to enlarge his palace grounds! But popular or not, the origin of the Church shows that its founder was a real person. It is impossible to explain it otherwise.

The Gospels show that Jesus was real. They represent a completely new type of literature, thrown up by the new movement. Nobody wrote Gospels before. There are four of them, and they were written by Jesus' followers and their associates. Much of the material clearly went the rounds by word of mouth before it got written down some thirty or forty years after Jesus' death. The Gospels are written from different perspectives by different men, but the figure they bring before us is manifestly the same. All of them have the spell of Jesus about them. He made such a fantastic impression on them that the normal categories of history and biography did not seem enough. They were impelled to start a completely new literary genre to do justice to this completely different man. Incidentally, in case anybody tells you that the Gospels have been messed around with and embroidered as the centuries have rolled on, you might be interested to know that the manuscript tradition is far stronger for our Gospels than it is for any other ancient book. Normally a thousand years or so separates the original from the oldest copy we possess. And normally there are only one or two ancient copies on which the whole text depends. With the Gospels we have manuscripts going back to within a hundred years of the originals, and there are literally hundreds of ancient copies written in a dozen languages. We can be absolutely sure that the Gospels have come down to us very much as they were written. They are as real and firm as the Jesus they present.

Ancient Roman historians show us that Jesus was real. That is very remarkable when you come to think about it, because these literary Romans were very superior creatures. Why should they bother about a peasant teacher who lived on the very edge of the map, in Judaea? Nevertheless some of them did bother. Pliny was the governor of Northern Turkey, right up by the Black Sea, in about A.D. 112. He wrote lots of letters to the Emperor, and they have survived. He tells us about the Christians, their numbers, their influence (sale of sacrificial victims for the pagan temples had dropped to nothing!) their worship (early in the morning with hymns to Christ as God) their loving and harmless lives, and their regrettable unwillingness to stop being Christians when he told them to! Many of them he executed, but the movement refused to lie down and die. You can read all about it in his *Epistles* 10: 96.

Another aristocratic Roman writer was Cornelius Tacitus, the Governor of the rich province of Asia Minor (our central and coastal Turkey). He writes of the way in which the Emperor Nero picked on the Christians as scapegoats for the Fire of Rome in A.D. 64. He tells of the incredible cruelty practised on them: some were clothed in the skins of wild beasts and torn apart by dogs, while others were covered with pitch and set alight at night in Nero's gardens. Tacitus felt sorry for them, but he did not like them. With well-bred distaste he notes, "The name 'Christian' comes to them from Christ, who was executed in the reign of Tiberius by the procurator Pontius Pilate; and the pernicious faith, suppressed for a while, broke out afresh and spread not only through Judaea, the source of the disease, but even throughout Rome itself where everything vile comes and is fêted" (*Annals* 15: 44). There is plenty of other Roman evidence that Jesus was a real person of recent date. The cities of Pompeii and Herculaneum were overwhelmed by a volcano in A.D. 79, and Christian mosaics, wall paintings, and inscriptions have been found there – also, in all probability, an early Christan chapel. Archaeology has also come up with a decree from the Emperor Tiberius (A.D. 14–38) or Claudius (A.D. 41–54), discovered in Nazareth which threatens with the death penalty anyone who disturbs tombs: it looks as if this is official reaction to Pilate's report of the empty tomb of Jesus. There can be no doubt in the mind of anyone who takes historical evidence seriously that Jesus actually lived and died in

Palestine under the governorship of Pontius Pilate which ended in A.D. 36.

The Jewish writers also show that Jesus was real. Christianity soon became a great threat to Judaism, and there is evidence to show that the very mention of Jesus was frowned on in Jewish documents. Nevertheless scattered through the Mishnah there are allusions like these. "Rabbi Eliezer said, 'Balaam looked forth and saw that there was a man, born of a woman, who would rise up and seek to make himself God, and cause the whole world to go astray.' " We read of his miracles, with the disparaging comment, "He learnt magic in Egypt." We read, too, of his death, "They hanged Jeshua of Nazareth on the eve of Passover." But the most surprising passage of all comes in Josephus, *Antiquities* 18: 3. Josephus was an influential Jewish refugee-general, writing in Rome in the 90s, and very keen to keep his nose clean and get the best deal possible for his conquered countrymen, who were smarting under the sack of Jerusalem in A.D. 70. So you would not expect him to say much about a controversial figure like Jesus. What, then, do you make of this? "And there arose about this time (i.e. Pilate's governorship) Jesus, a wise man, if indeed we should call him a man; for he was a doer of marvellous deeds, a teacher of men who receive the truth with pleasure. He won over many Jews and also many Greeks. This man was the Messiah. When Pilate had condemned him to the cross at the instigation of our leaders, those who had loved him from the first did not cease. For he appeared to them on the third day alive again, as the holy prophets had predicted, and said many other wonderful things about him. And even now the race of Christians, so named after him, has not yet died out."

When you get a piece as explicit as that in an anti-Christian writer it is pretty shattering. No wonder lots of people have attacked the text. Nevertheless this passage is there in all the manuscripts of Josephus. Some of it may well be ironic. But there can be no doubt from this Jewish evidence that Jesus was a real historical person. And notice how we have allusions, scattered throughout this hostile testimony, to his unusual birth ("born of a woman" means "conceived out of wedlock" in Jewish culture), his date, his disciples, his miracles (although assigned to the devil's agency!), his claims ("seek to make himself God"), his messiahship, his death on the cross, his reported resurrection, and his continuing impact on society through his followers. That is a great deal to have gleaned from sources who, for different reasons, were so strongly opposed to Christianity. Wherever you look, then, in the ancient records, be they Christian, archaeological, Roman, or Jewish, you find the same message. Jesus was real: no doubt about it. Moreover Jesus *is* real: he is still in business. And just because he is real, just because he is there, he is well worth bothering about. After all, we do not date our whole era by a myth!

4

Bother because he is the Ideal

DID YOU EVER see Pelé play football? He drew thousands to the stands whenever he played. His artistry was supreme. He was, perhaps, the greatest attacking footballer the world has ever seen. The ideal, if you like.

Football may not be your thing. What is? If it's literature, would you not give a lot to spend a few hours with William Shakespeare? If it's politics, you'd learn such a lot about leadership from Augustus Caesar. We have approximations to the ideal in every walk of life, but they all have their failings, and they fade as the years pass by.

But is there anyone who is the ideal not merely for football, literature or politics, but for living? Is there anyone who has shown us what humanity is really capable of? Is there an ideal man?

Fifty years ago it was fashionable to suppose that we were developing towards a race of Supermen: the ideal lay before us, and close at hand. Now, in the light of the Second World War and all that has followed it, such optimism looks particularly dated. These days we vaguely hope that the ideal may come from Mars in a space ship. The ideal still lies before us, even if not so close at hand.

But we are all busy looking in the wrong direction. The ideal has come. The perfect life has been lived. We are no longer able to plead ignorance of what it means to be fully human. In Jesus, the real historical Jesus, we see the heights to which man can rise. In him we see perfection.

Take the life of Jesus as recorded in the Gospels. It is so superb, and yet so unexpected, that nobody could have made it up – let alone four evangelists working independently from one another! That life is perfect: there's no other word for it.

Think of the influence of that life. Wherever you look in art, music and literature you find that many of the greatest compositions have concerned Jesus of Nazareth. Think of medicine, education and humane government. There are places in the world where atheist regimes are to the fore in these three areas (though jolly few of them, when you come to tot them up); but in every instance the first people to bother about the bodies and minds of men, as well as their souls have been the Christians. The ideals of Jesus have not always been followed in Western Europe. But those ideals have shaped what Europe is. This is also the case in Australia and in both North and South America. In Africa the biggest single cultural influence is Jesus, and the growth of the Church far outruns the growth of the population of that whole continent.

Think of the appeal of that life. It has fired the idealism and touched the hearts of all types of men, all over the world, all down the centuries. It has appealed equally to bosses and to servants, to soldiers and to monks, to stone age cultures and to sophisticated professors. It has appealed to downtrodden and to prosperous alike. And it has never done so by condoning their failings or feeding their self-esteem. Always that life has chal-

lenged men, even as it has appealed to them. A most un-
comfortable ideal: but all nations of the world and all types of
men and women within them have confessed that he is the
ideal. Not only has there been no better. It is impossible to
conceive of any advance on Jesus of Nazareth.

Think of the balance of that life. The perfect balance between action and reflection, between masculine virtues and
those generally associated with women. The mixture of gentle-
ness and toughness, of compassion and straight talk, of gaiety
and seriousness is phenomenal. Here was a man who was as
much at home in a hovel or a palace, with a penitent call-girl, a
truculent fisherman or a selfish governor. And, incredibly, he is
always quietly in command of every situation: perfectly bal-
anced.

Think of the inspiration of that life. The life and example of
Jesus have sustained the persecuted believers during the first
three centuries, acted as a beacon to the monks in the dark ages,
tamed the cruelty of the Vikings, conquered the conquering
Normans – just see how many churches they left all over the
place! Christ was the inspiration behind the gallantry of the
knights in the days of chivalry. A rediscovery of Christ led to
the Reformation. In the eighteenth century the vision of Jesus,
Jesus only, so dominated men like Whitfield and Wesley that
the whole face of England was changed inside a generation
from brutish, drunken atheism. In the days of the Industrial
Revolution too little attention was paid to him and too much to
profits: the bitterness in industrial relations to which this led is
still with us. But even so, the Trade Unions were founded
largely as a result of Christ and his influence and ideals. Jesus
stands behind the Tolpuddle martyrs. It was he who inspired a
world-wide missionary movement in the nineteenth century
which fired men to go and tell the heathen about the Saviour
even if they should themselves perish in the telling – as many of
them did. It is Jesus to whom many of the Liberation move-
ments of the twentieth century are looking for their inspiration:
Jesus, the non-establishment man, the man for others, the
leader who gave his own life. If you had asked Ghandi, the
father of modern India, who was his model, he would un-
doubtedly have replied "Jesus". There are, in fact, signs at
present that both Islam and Hinduism are looking to Jesus as in
some way the ideal human being. The truth of the matter is
that there are no serious competitors. Jesus is the ideal.

Is not that a very strong reason why you should bother with

Jesus? He is not merely the greatest man ever, he is the ideal
for all men to follow. Wouldn't you think, then, that men would
crowd round him, aching to be his followers? Just as football
fans crowd round Pelé? But they don't, do they? And they
didn't when he was around on earth either. Now isn't that a
very odd thing? Does it not suggest that we are terrified by the
ideal? We are afraid he might want to change some areas of our
lives which are not ideal at all – but which we cling onto for all
we are worth. So it is much easier, and safer, and more
comfortable to turn our back on him and say "Why bother
about Jesus? What's so special about him?"

5

Bother because his character is the greatest

FOR MORE THAN a decade the Beatles in one sphere and Mu-
hammed Ali in another have been proclaiming themselves "the
greatest". Difficult as it is to get to the top in singing, it is much
harder in character, and as we saw in the last chapter, that is
what Jesus has done. He is without doubt the greatest, noblest,
most lovely character ever.

He was prayerful without being pious. The Gospels are full
of his warm, natural intercourse with his Father in prayer, and
equally full of his friendship with those who never darkened the
door of a synagogue. If there had been any touch of primness,

of "holier-than-thou" about him, the ordinary folks would have
kept well clear.

He was vital without being hearty. There is a strong sense of
movement about the Gospel story which springs from Jesus
himself. His straight and powerful language, his sheer energy,
his commitment to individuals in need. No half measures about
him. But never a touch of heartiness.

He was peaceful without being idle. Not many energetic men
are peaceful. They are opposite qualities. But Jesus combined
them. He was utterly at peace all the time: he called it the
peace of God. No disaster, no interruption robbed him of that
inner serenity. And though intense pressure led him away to
rest for short periods, he was back in the battle in a short time,
radiating peace.

He exuded love without sentimentality. Love that could
make a prostitute weep, that could dandle little children on his
knee, that could embrace the untouchables. He said that
"greater love has no man than this; that a man should lay down
his life for his friends". Well, he even improved on that astonishing goal: he laid down his life for his enemies.

He was modest and yet authoritative. On the one hand he
owned no money, never looked for praise, put on no airs, acted
in constant and deep dependence of God. On the other he spoke
about spiritual things as one who *knew*. "Truly, truly, I tell
you" was his characteristic way of address, and men recognised
that he taught with astonishing authority although he had never
been to college.

He had a genius for friendship, but it never turned to favour-
itism. Time after time in the Gospels you find Jesus talking to a
single Pharisee, a blind man, a beggar, a lame man, a mourning
widow, a Roman soldier. A tremendous variety of needs, and he
cared about them all so much that each one must have felt that
he was the only person that mattered to Jesus for the time
being. That's quite right: he was. His friendship with the
women who accompanied him, his friendship with the dozen
disciples who left house and home to stay with him — this is
one of the most attractive traits of character.

Actually, it would not be difficult to write a whole book on
the character of Jesus. It would be a long book, because every
conceivable virtue known to man is there in him. I've just given
a few samples.

But now I want to look at the other side. He did not merely
have all the virtues, he had none of the vices. At least, I do not

know of any. I have only ever heard three being suggested, and
none of them hold water.

Some protest that he used violence in kicking crooked
traders and cheapjacks out of the Temple when they had
"turned my Father's house into a den of robbers". I am not sure
that I would have thought it wrong if he had used that thong of
cords he had in his hands! But we are not told that he did. He
just turfed them out.

The second moan is that he lost his temper with the fig tree
and cursed it petulantly. Not a bit of it. His cursing of the fig
tree was an acted parable. The fig tree had for centuries been a
symbol of the Jewish nation. Jesus had come to Jerusalem and
found that they rejected him. He had found no fruit on the fig
tree of Israel. He pronounced on it the judgement of God, and
that judgement awaits us all, so we had better not be too high
and mighty about it. In historical terms it took place just 40
years later, when the Roman legions smashed the Holy City
(which specialised in killing the prophets) to smithereens.

The third complaint I have heard against Jesus' character is
that he had no sense of humour. I find that hilarious! How can
any man with a perfectly straight face tell his very smug and
pious hearers that they must remove a whacking great plank
from their own eye before they can see clearly to pull the tiniest
speck out of their brother's eye? Can you imagine him sitting as
solemn as a lord while he ticked the Pharisees off for their
punctilious care in straining out any unclean thing, like a gnat,
from their wine — whilst not realising that they were swallow-
ing the most whopping unclean beast in the book, a camel?
Don't tell me Jesus hadn't got a sense of humour. Read the
Gospels and see.

Having cleared that little lot out of the way, let me get back
to the main point. And a very remarkable one it is, too. *Jesus
had no vices*. Jesus never did anything wrong. The Gospels
never praise him: but they never give a single example of anything for which he had to say "My mistake" or "So sorry".
Those sorts of incidents did not take place. He told his disciples
to say "Forgive us our trespasses" each time they said the
Lord's Prayer, but that was the prayer the Lord taught
them – not the one he used himself. His claim was "I do
always those things which please Him" (John 8.9). He seems
to have been conscious of no cloud between him and his
heavenly Father. Remarkable, and all the more remarkable in
one who was so quick to spot hypocrisy in the prayers of the

religious, so much showmanship in the donations of the "generous", so many lustful, murderous thoughts lurking under respectable exteriors which were so ready to condemn adultery and murder in others. How could a man as perceptive as this possibly not have apologised to God in his prayers? The only answer I can see is this. He did not say "Sorry" for his misdeeds, *because he did not have any.* If you say "That is fantastic", I agree. We are talking about "the greatest", remember? His life was not just the greatest: it was a moral miracle.

It's an interesting thing, but those who liked him and those who didn't both bore witness to his perfection of character. There's a marvellous passage in John 8.39ff where Jesus is hinting that he is older than Abraham (who had died two thousand years earlier) and that he shares the nature and the glory of God. They are hopping mad, good monotheists that they are, and rush to deal with him in the time-honoured method for disposing of blasphemers, by hurling stones at him. But Jesus gives them pause. He says, "Which of you can point to anything wrong in my life?" (v. 46). No surely that is asking for it. Could you get away with it? Of course not. Your friends, let alone your enemies, would be only too quick to point out a thousand and one things you had done wrong. But these people were tongue-tied. There was nothing to say.

You find just the same at his trial. They try for hours to find some charge that would stick. And they fail, conclusively. They know quite well that the accusations they are rigging won't stand the cold light of day, and they give it up as a bad job. In the end they ask him if he is God's long awaited Messiah; he says, "That is your way of putting it," and they give three jumps for joy and do him for blasphemy. That shows how pushed they were to find anything wrong in him. It was the same with Pontius Pilate, who three times during the most remarkable trial in history declared his prisoner innocent, and then handed him over to the execution squad. Even Pilate's wife could not get to sleep the night before, and sent a message to him while he was hearing the trial saying, "Have nothing to do with the blood of this innocent man." But he didn't listen: he was afraid that clemency would lose him his job. But he inwardly agreed with his wife's assessment of Jesus. So did the centurion who was in charge of the execution. So did one of the men being killed alongside him. They all unite to say with one voice: "This man is completely innocent."

"Ah," you may say. "But these folk did not get close enough to him to see the flaws." Well, listen to some who did. Peter was as close to him as anyone, and he sums the situation up like this: "He committed no wrong. No guile was found on his lips. When he was reviled he did not revile again. When he suffered he did not threaten, but he trusted to him who judges justly" (1 Peter 2: 22f). That shows how he regarded his Master. The writer to the Hebrews was equally clear about it all. "This is the sort of high priest we needed: holy, blameless, unstained, separated from sinners" (7: 26). This is the sort of high priest God provided for us. "He was tempted in all points just like we are; yet without sin" (4: 15). John got closer to him, perhaps, than anyone else, and John has precisely the same assessment. "If we say that we have no sin, we deceive ourselves and the truth is not in us . . . but in him is no sin" (1 John 1: 8, 3: 5). The evidence is identical, whatever quarter you look. And it is conclusive.

In Jesus of Nazareth you find a perfect character, the only one in all history who has never done anything wrong.

Perhaps that helps us to understand a little more the problem I mentioned at the end of the previous chapter: the way we fight shy of Jesus, whereas we would cheerfully flock round any other great man. The truth of the matter is that his life so puts ours to shame that we are deeply embarrassed. John puts it like this. "Light has come into the world (with the coming of Jesus) and men loved darkness rather than light because their deeds were evil." (John 3: 1). That puts a rather different complexion on our "Why bother with Jesus?" attitude, does it not? It shows that it is not only foolish but guilty. If the light of his perfect life turns us off, then that says something very clear about our sinful lives. It indicates that a big change is needed. Jesus talked about that. He called it conversion. Read on: we shall be coming to it.

6

Bother because of his offer

ONE OF THE striking differences between Christianity and the other religions is that the others all start with the assumption that God is known. Christianity does not. Jesus says that nobody knows God in the personal sense of Father except himself; and he alone can bring people into that intimate relationship (Matt. 11: 27f). He then follows that up with one of the most marvellous offers that have ever passed the lips of man, "Come to me, all who labour and are heavy laden, and I will give you rest."

What a fantastic offer. I find three or four heavy laden ones an enormous burden to cope with. Jesus invites all! And in many ways that is the heart of his teaching. It is not primarily demand, though demand is there. It is primarily offer, free offer. We have got a bit cynical about free offers, because so often they aren't free at all; there's a catch in them somehow. But the very fact that the free offer business is so widespread in the supermarkets reminds us that a genuine free gift is one of the most attractive things in the world. That is what the religion of Jesus is all about.

"See here," he says. "You do not know God, although a lot of you are very religious. You are strangers to him. You are, frankly, lost. Well, listen to me. God cares about that. I know, because I know him in a way none of you do. He is my heavenly Father. I talk to him in the same family way as you chat to your dad." (His special word for the Father, "Abba" means "dear Dad". It was never used between man and God until Jesus used it.) Would you not like to be in the family, and be able to share your life with the Father like that?

"What's more, God is King. He is king of the whole earth, but a lot of his kingdom is unruly and rebellious. Let's be honest about it. You are like that, are you not? Your heart is a rebel against him: you are too busy doing your own thing to bother about what he wants. But with me it is different. I am not only the perfect Servant of the King: I do always what pleases him. But I am also the embodiment of his Kingdom. I come with his authority to represent him, and show in my life and teaching what God's way of leadership is. His Kingdom is one where love is supreme; where trust replaces suspicion, generosity replaces hatred, and mutual service replaces bossing people around. I want to show you the attractiveness of life in the Kingdom. I want to teach you the law of the Kingdom: so why not take time off now to read my Sermon on the Mount? It is in Matthew chapters five to seven. It will give you a bird's eye view of what life in God's Kingdom could be like. And notice the end bit. It is only by entering through me, by knowing me, by building your life on me, that you will ever discover what his Kingdom can mean for you personally. I tell you about God's Kingdom. I represent that Kingdom in my own life. I am the way in to that Kingdom. So 'Come to me, all who labour and are heavy laden, and I will give you rest.' "

Jesus thought in pictures. So do most of us – which is why we find the bureaucratic government forms so difficult to fill in. Let some of these pictures give you a glimpse of what he offers.

Do you want to know what God's Kingdom is like, said Jesus? I will tell you. For some it is like a ploughman slogging along day in day out with his oxen, trying to keep a straight furrow – as bored as can be. Suddenly, one day, his ploughshare hits a box hidden in the ground. He gets down, wrenches the lid off it, and out cascades a heap of shimmering jewels. You can just imagine how that farm labourer pawns all his belongings in order to raise enough money to make that field, with its box of treasure, his own!

For others it is like a pearl fancier. Imagine a very experienced merchant who has been in the pearl business all his life, and knows a thing or two. One day he finds a pearl which takes his breath away. For size, brilliance and sheer perfection he has never, in all his experience, seen anything to compare with it. He manages to hide his excitement, haggles over the price, and once it is agreed goes off and sells all his stock of pearls because life would not be worth living for him if he did not possess that pearl of great price.

There you have it. Entering God's Kingdom is like finding treasure, like discovering the pearl that puts all other pearls in the shade. Did you realise that? Probably not. Like me, you may have thought it was a matter of trying hard and doing good things and going to church and all manner of dull and dreary occupations. That just shows how effective the propaganda from His Infernal Eminence has been. Because the life that is shared with Jesus Christ is the most joyful and rewarding and full life a man can possibly live. Did he not say "I am come that you might have life, and have it in all its fullness" (John 10: 11)? Yes, entering the Kingdom is infinitely satisfying. You may come upon it all of a sudden while slogging along the road of life, feeling that everything is a bit jaded and dull and a bore. You may have been seeking it for years as you ploughed through a variety of philosophies or religions or drug trips. People come upon it by either path. Once they see what is offered, the shrewd ones realise it is the most important thing in the world. They are willing for any sacrifice, in order to possess it.

Another of Jesus' pictures puts it very clearly. Think of God as a rich king, who has decided to have the most marvellous wedding reception for his son. He does two remarkable things. First, he sends out invitations. Many of those invited turn it down: so he invites all and sundry to come to his banquet – folk from the streets, the brothels, the middle-class homes, the ghettos. That is what God is like. Willing to have anyone to his great feast of the Christian life. He makes the offer. He provides the good things. He sends the invitations. God is not a cold Judge saying "Go." He is the man who throws a party and says "Come."

But the second remarkable thing in the story is this. The King provides a superb banqueting robe for all his guests. They exchange it for their ordinary clothes when they come inside the door. It would be awful if the banquet were spoiled by some folk boasting in their fine clothes while others come in

dirty and ragged off the streets. So God makes provision for us
all to enjoy his banquet without any trace of embarrassment at
the mess our own lives have been in, or of pride in our own
achievements. We all come in on the level. We all wear the
perfect dress of his forgiveness, his acceptance. Otherwise we
don't get in at all. Actually there is a bit about that in the story
Jesus told. One man slipped in with his own clothes on, re-
fusing the wedding robe, claiming, no doubt, that his own
dinner jacket was quite good enough. And when the King came
in and saw the guests, this chap stuck out like a sore thumb. So
the King went and asked him why he had refused the proffered
wedding garment. The man had nothing to say. Guess what
happened to him? He was thrown out on his ear. God is not
going to have stuck-up people ruining his Kingdom. We enter
it as forgiven men, forgiven by him at his expense and nothing
to do with our merits – or we do not enter at all.

Such is the amazing teaching of Jesus. Free forgiveness, free
membership of God's family – the God I have neglected and
snubbed and pretended did not exist. And that life of love and
peace and joy and good relationships is a party, a real banquet.
It cost him everything to prepare. It costs me nothing to accept
– except my pride. For I have to take it as a gift, not dream I
can earn it by trying a bit harder, going to church a bit more
often, or subscribing to the Archbishop's Fund for Disabled
Dogs.

Have you got the message? Or is it still too mind-boggling to
take in? If so, listen to this. Do you remember your old mum
the day she lost her engagement ring? Every drawer was turned
out. Every room was swept out. Every nook and cranny was
searched. And then the ring turned up! Tears ran down her
face. She hugged you. She ran round to the neighbours to tell
them. She was quite literally jumping for joy. Now that, believe it or not, is God's attitude to us. When we get "lost" from
him, he isn't furious with us: he doesn't say "Wait till I catch
up with that rebel Bill". He loves us so much that he does
everything he possibly can to seek us out, draw us back, woo us
to the life of love in his home that we have foolishly thrown
away. And when we come back – wow! "There is joy in heaven
over one sinner that comes back" (Luke 15: 10).

In a companion story which Jesus told about the runaway
boy who left home, wasted his livelihood, and then began to feel
the pinch, there is a similar happy ending. The boy comes back,
full of fears about his reception, and finds his old dad is already

out looking for him, scanning the skyline day by day to see if there is any sign of his return. He runs out to meet him, gives him a complete new outfit of clothes, and orders a great banquet and dance of celebration "for this my son was dead, and is alive again, was lost and is found" (Luke 15: 24).

That is what God is like, so Jesus tells us. Now do you see why Christianity cannot go along with the other religions in supposing that we know what God is like? Who on earth could have supposed that God is that loving, that generous? Who would ever have dreamed that he would welcome rebels back into his Kingdom for free, that he would adopt into his family urchins like us? But that *is* what God is like. And Jesus came to tell us. "No man has ever seen God: the only Son, who is in the bosom of the Father, he has made him known" (John 1: 18). And when a free offer of that quality and magnitude is going, I think there is good reason to bother about Jesus. Search all the religions of the world. You will not find in any of them a similar offer.

7

Bother because of his claims

WHO IS THIS Jesus who says "Come to me and I will give you rest"? Who does he think he is?

Good question. Let's see who he thinks he is. Ask anyone you stop in the street and I'll bet he will say something like this: "Jesus Christ? Yeah, a great chap. Good teacher. A really wonderful man." Now examine the actual teaching of this wonderful teacher, this really great man, and you find a very different picture emerging.

He didn't lay a lot of emphasis on his teaching. Other people did, and were astonished at its originality and power. But he played his teaching pretty cool. "My teaching is not mine but his who sent me," he said. "I do nothing on my own authority, but speak thus as the Father taught me."

He didn't lay a lot of emphasis on his goodness. Indeed, when one man ventured to address him, somewhat patronisingly, as "Good Master", he answered him very firmly: "Why do you call me good? There is one good, and that is God." Goodness in its ultimate form does not belong to man, but to God. Perhaps he was trying to stretch the mind of the questioner and make him see the truth.

For the truth is, according to Jesus' claims, that he is not merely a man. He is that. He was born like us, was hungry and thirsty like us, tired like us. Like us he could grieve, he could bleed, he could die. Human through and through. But something more. Not even a great prophet or a wonderful teacher or a fabulous character. Something more.

He claimed to live a sinless life. As we have already seen, he could look at an angry crowd, angry because he was implicitly claiming to share God's very nature, and ask them, "Which of you can point to anything wrong in my life?" I don't know whether that question is the more amazing – or the fact that none of them could give a reply! But in any case, no mere man could have lived a spotless life. Jesus did.

He claimed to be the way of God. Not a way, but *the* way. Not to teach the way, but to be the way. "I am the way, the truth, the life. No man comes to the Father but by me" (John 14: 6). Or take that verse we considered in the last chapter: "All things have been delivered to me by my Father. And no one knows the Son except the Father, and no one knows the Father except the Son and any one to whom the Son chooses to reveal him." (Matt. 11: 27). Nobody has ever made claims like that before and backed them, as Jesus did, by a quality of life, a love, a balance, an influence like his. No mere man ever made such claims. Jesus did.

He claimed to give life to people. Not just to tell them about where they could get it or improve it or deepen it, but to give life. "I give to them eternal life, and they shall never perish, neither shall any one snatch them out of my hand. My Father who gave them to me is greater than all, and no one is able to snatch them out of my Father's hand. I and the Father are one" (John 10: 30). Can you imagine anyone in his right mind making claims like that if he were merely a man? Jesus made them.

He claimed to be able to forgive sins. On one occasion he was teaching in a house and the people were jammed tight around him. So some bright jokers had the idea of taking the roof off and letting down one of their paralysed friends whom they hoped Jesus would heal. Jesus looked at the man, swinging there on a bed with a rope attached to each corner. It was perfectly obvious what the man's need was. He was paralysed. But Jesus rarely did the obvious. He said to the man, "Your sins are forgiven you." Now the room was full of theologians. They were furious. "Who can forgive sins, but God alone?" was their muttered question. Who indeed? That is the very point Jesus wanted them to take in. So he said to them. "In order that you may know that the Son of Man (his name for himself) has power on earth to forgive sins" – he turned to the paralysed man – "Take up your bed and walk." The man did just that, to the amazement of the crowd – and the discomfiture of the theologians. Jesus claimed the power to forgive sins – God's special prerogative – and he backed that claim with mighty cures. This was not an isolated instance. We find Jesus telling a prostitute that her sins, which were many, are forgiven; a publican that he can go down to his house acquitted; or a dying murderer that he would go to heaven. We might well ask, like the theologians round the paralysed man, "Who can forgive sins, but God alone?" (Mark 2: 7). Jesus did.

He claimed the right to receive men's worship. This is really staggering, in view of his humility and his sense of dependence on his heavenly Father. No merely good man would do that. We find both Peter and Paul in the Acts of the Apostles being offered worship by ignorant pagans. Both of them immediately recoiled in horror from the suggestion. But Jesus accepted it as his due. On one occasion after a miraculous catch of fish, Peter fell at this feet and said "Depart from me, for I am a sinful man, O Lord" (Luke 5: 8). Jesus did nothing to deter him. On another occasion, after his resurrection, Jesus found the doubter, Thomas, in a heap at his feet, worshipping him in the most explicit terms, "My Lord and My God." Again he accepted it quite naturally and merely encouraged Thomas to trust without seeing in future. Can you think of any religious leader acting like that? Neither can I. Jesus did.

He claimed to be the judge of all mankind. Do you remember that famous story of the sheep and the goats? Jesus said that at the end of time he would divide men into two groups, as a shepherd separates sheep and goats in his flock. *Jesus* would do it! He had claimed elsewhere that the Father had committed all judgement to him. And at the end of the Sermon on the Mount he had made it clear that only if men entered through him would they get inside the Kingdom: only if they knew him would they find a welcome; only if he was their foundation would their building stand. Is it possible to make more shattering claims than these? The destiny of a man will be determined by his attitude to Jesus. Of what mere man could that he said? Jesus maintained it.

There are other claims which make it clear to me that in Jesus I hear God addressing me, and not only a man. For one thing he says that *he will lay down his life for the straying sheep of the world* (John 10: 15). Or, to change the metaphor, Jesus will "give his life as a ransom for many" (Mark 10: 45). Who but God could do that? To give his life as a counterweight to all the death in our spoiled lives. That is too great a task for any man: if Jesus does it for the world, then he must be, as his very name suggests, "God the Saviour" at work. Another of his claims which leaves me breathless is that *his words will never pass away.* "Heaven and earth shall pass away but my words shall not pass away" was his claim (Mark 13: 31). It has come true. The Bible containing his words is the world's best seller and it is translated into far more languages than any other book. Does this not suggest that one more than man was speaking?

But the really ultimate claim of Jesus is that *he would raise men up in the last day*, and that the key to eternal life lay in relationship with him who was about to die and rise again. On the way to death himself he showed himself Lord of death by raising Lazarus from the tomb. That was an illustration of what his death would do. The very night before he died he encouraged his followers with an assurance that makes Socrates look pale. "Let not your hearts be troubled. Believe in God, believe also in me. In my Father's house are many rooms. If it were not so I would have told you. I go to prepare a place for you" (John 14:1f). Even death could not shackle him.

Who is this that made such claims? A sinless life, teaching that would last for ever, the power to forgive sins, to accept worship, to be the final judge of men, to give his life a ransom for us, to raise us up at the last day. Who is this? He comes to us not merely as a man, not even the greatest man who ever lived. Not as a great teacher, or a wonderful healer. He comes to us with the authority of almighty God his heavenly Father. He shares his Father's nature, his Father's power, his Father's finality. He is not merely man, but a chip of the divine block. When we face up to him we face up to the human face of God. That's why we need to bother with Jesus.

8

Bother because he loves you

SHE HOLDS YOU tight and murmurs in your ear "Darling, I love you." Marvellous. It makes you feel very good. But will it last? Or is it a passing feeling that may be gone tomorrow and by next year may be murmured into somebody else's ear? We have almost forgotten what real love is like nowadays, because we are so hooked on the emotional feelings that go with it.

Real love is tough. Real love is lasting. Real love is unselfish. Real love hates to see blemishes in the beloved. Real love can put up with anything. Real love is willing to suffer for the loved one. Real love is willing to die for him.

That is the sort of love Jesus Christ has for us lot. And it is not because he finds us attractive. He doesn't. Has it ever struck you how petty, how repulsive, how foul we must look to the perfectly sinless eyes of Jesus? He loves us not because he finds us attractive, not because we deserve it, but simply because he is love. Listen to the way the New Testament stresses it time and again. 'God so loved the world that he gave his only Son that whosoever believes in him should not perish but have everlasting life" (John 3: 16). "God shows his love for us in that while we were still sinners Christ died for us" (Romans 5: 8). "God is love. In this is the love of God made manifest, that he sent his Son to be the remedy for the dirt of our sins" (1 John 4: 8f). And an exiled Christian leader, John, condemned to the mines in the island of Patmos, is full of praise for the love that has met him and changed his life. "Unto him who loves us and has freed us from our sins by his blood . . . to him be glory and dominion for ever and ever" (Rev. 1: 5). But perhaps the most moving expression of what it means to be reached personally by that love of God is found on St. Paul's lips, "The Son of God loved me, and gave himself for me" (Galatians 2: 20). It is a marvellous thing to be loved. It somehow purifies you, it ennobles you, it makes you carry your head high. You want everyone to know about it. Your heart sings. Someone has thought you worth loving. And that is one of the most marvellous things about the Christian life. The Lord himself has thought you and me worth loving.

But how do you *know*? And how do you know he loves *me*? Those are the burning questions. Mercifully the New Testament gives a clear answer to them. We do not have to remain in doubt or suspense about so important a matter.

What is the most important mark or symbol of Christianity? The cross, of course. And that cross gives us the answer to our problem. It is an answer that the most profound thinker has never got to the bottom of, but it is an answer which can be perfectly clear, in outline, to a child. That nanny who wrote the famous hymn "There is a green hill, far away" for her children, had got the message very clear:

> There was no other good enough
> To pay the price of sin
> He only could unlock the gate
> Of heaven and let us in.
>
> He died that we might be forgiven
> He died to make us good,
> That we might go at last to heaven
> Saved by his precious blood.

Yes, the cross of Jesus Christ is the proof, the unanswerable
proof, of how much he loves us. He loved us enough to be
mocked, despised, betrayed, given the cat-o'-nine-tails, and
nailed alive to a ghastly great chunk of wood before being hung
up amid the flies and the heat and the agony to die in excru-
ciating pain in however many hours it took. When I look at
Calvary I can have no doubt that he loves me, with a love
stronger than death.

But why did he go there? What was the point? Could he not
show his love in some less gruesome way? Yes, perhaps he
could. But he did not go to the cross simply to show us how
much he loved us. That was part of it, and a most important
part of it. Like a magnet it has drawn men to Jesus ever since.
But there was more to Calvary than that. He had a job to do on
that terrible gallows.

To describe that job very bluntly, he went there to save us.
We needed saving so badly that no other way was possible.
That's an old-fashioned word, but we still use it. If you were
washed over a weir in a river, you would need saving. If you
were in a burning house, you would need saving. If you were
broke with a thousand pound debt on your hands, you would
need somebody to step in and save you. That is the sort of
rescue the New Testament has in mind when its writers say
that Jesus saved mankind on the cross. He saved us from
drowning in the alienation into which we had slipped, away
from God. He saved us from being destroyed in the burning
house of our own selfishness. He saved us from the enormous
debt of our failures before God when we had nothing to pay
with: he stepped in, and paid it himself for us.

You say, "I still don't see it." Right, let me turn you to the
simplest and most profound explanation of the cross and its
meaning that I know. It comes in the first letter of someone
who was there on the edge of the execution crowd that first
Good Friday, Simon Peter. Why did he die, Simon? You ought
to know. "Christ once suffered for sins, the just for the unjust,
that he might bring us to God" (1 Peter 3: 18). That is why. On
the cross he suffered unspeakable agonies. Why did he bother?
To bring us to God: that was his supreme purpose in coming to
this earth at all. What was in the way? Our *sins*, of course. Our
selfishness, lust, hate, greed, meanness, pride and all the rest of
the horrid things in our lives. They acted like a great wall
between us and God. We couldn't see to the other side. We
didn't even know for sure if there was another side, and if

anyone was there. But on the cross Jesus suffered to get that sin wall pulled down. He achieved it by allowing the wall to fall on himself. *The just for the unjust*: that was it. He, the just one, took the place of us the unjust, paying our debts, bearing our load, serving our sentence. He did it so that we could be well and truly forgiven by God without for one moment denying his justice. It was all fair: the Lord himself had borne the penalty in our place.

Once you see that, it takes your breath away. Did he love me that much? Yes, Calvary proves it. What, me? Yes, you. He loved you that much. "The Son of God loved me and gave himself for me" sings Paul, the rebel turned disciple. He never ceased to wonder at it. Can you blame him? Isn't your own heart beginning to thrill at the thought that the Maker of the heavens and earth should love you enough to go to those lengths to save you from the results of your own stupid selfishness?

That sets a man free, that does. It puts a new song in his mouth and a new spring in his step. The Son of God loved me and gave himself for me. What a value that sets on little me. What a Lover the Lord must be. And I can be sure that I am forgiven because the thing has been settled once for all on that cruel – yet utterly glorious – cross.

You will notice that I have not attempted to give any human illustrations of what happened on that cross. There aren't any. For a love which sacrifices itself not for its friends but for its enemies has no parallel in our world. You will find no analogy of a sea captain going down with his ship or a mother sacrificing herself for her baby compares with it for one moment. You will not find anything in the other religions that remotely compares with it. It is utterly and gloriously unique. There is nothing in the whole wide world like the love of God for sinners. That is why you should bother with Jesus. He loves you so much that he was willing to go through all that for you. Can you look him in the eye, as he stretches out his nail-pierced hands to you in welcome, and say "Why should I bother about you?"

9

Bother because he conquered death

IF JESUS WAS just a marvellous person who lived a long time ago and loved us enough to go to a peculiarly unpleasant form of death – then it might be permissible to ignore him. After all, we have to look to the future, not be bound by the past. But if he rose from the grave, that puts things in an entirely different light. It means that one man has broken the death barrier. One man knows from personal experience what is on the other side. One man is qualified to guide us over the chilly flood of death. One man, unlike all others before and since, has been "defined as Son of God by the resurrection" (Rom. 1: 4). If that is true, then there is no possible excuse for ignoring him. If that is true, he towers above all other religious leaders, healers and teachers of mankind. Who else has risen from the dead?

But is it true? Did he leave that tomb on the first Easter Day? It is, at first sight, most unlikely. Dead men are not in the habit of leaving their graves. But wait a moment. Any dead men we know about have all succumbed to the human disease of sin and failure. We do not know what would happen when a perfect example of the species died. There haven't been any, apart from Jesus! We are in no position to say that he could not have broken the bands of death. So we had better examine the evidence. And the evidence that he rose is very strong indeed. So strong that although attempts have been made to crack it ever since the first century, no single alternative explanation has ever survived for long. They simply don't bear critical investigation. If you are interested in following this up, you might care to look at a leading lawyer's assessment, Professor Sir Norman Anderson's *The Evidence for the Resurrection.* Or if you don't like lawyers, see what a journalist made of it in Frank Morrison's *Who Moved the Stone?* I've had a go at it myself in *Man Alive.* There is obviously not space to go into the details here, but the broad outlines can be stated very simply.

First, let us get it quite clear that Jesus was dead. Dead beyond any shadow of doubt. He was certified as dead by the centurion in charge of the execution squad. He was recognised as dead by Pilate, the governor (who gave permission for a friend to bury his body). And the crowning proof is that when a spear was thrust into his side under his heart in order to make sure he was dead, out came what an eyewitness called "blood and water" (John 19: 34ff). Obviously the scientific explanation of this was unknown to men of those times, but the diagnosis is clear. Dark blood and light serum came from the body of Jesus, and the separation of clot from serum in the blood is the strongest medical proof that the patient is dead. So don't swallow any of the "swoon" theories which imagine that Jesus was not quite dead but recovered in the cool of the tomb! He was dead all right. But did he stay that way? Consider four factors.

Consider the rise of the Christian church. It began at Easter, when the followers of Jesus were dispirited, scattered and crestfallen. Their leader from whom they hoped such great things had met an untimely and disgraceful end. What could have turned them into a force which rocked the Roman Empire? They had one answer for it. That "this Jesus, whom you crucified, God raised up, and we are witnesses of it" (Acts 2: 32). Moreover the Church had three things from the start which underline this conviction that Jesus was risen. They had two sacraments, baptism and the Lord's Supper. In baptism the believer went down into the water and up the other side: this symbolised his union with Jesus in death and resurrection. In the Lord's Supper they not only recalled his death with gratitude but exulted in his risen presence as they "broke bread with gladness". Neither sacrament would have been conceivable had the resurrection of Jesus not lain at the very foundation of their belief. It was the same with the third innovation, Sunday. The Christians are from the outset found keeping the first day of the week special, instead of the seventh, as the Jews had done. Why? Because God's work of new creation in raising Jesus from the dead on the first day of the week seemed to them even more significant than his completing the work of creation and resting on the seventh day of the week. Once again, you see, the resurrection is absolutely central.

Consider the empty grave of Jesus. On all sides it is agreed that the tomb was empty on the first Easter Day. If it were not, the Jews could very easily have silenced the Christians when they first began to preach the risen Jesus. They could have said, "Far from being risen, he is decaying in the grave round the corner." But much as they would have loved to say this, and so nip the new movement in the bud, they were not able to say anything of the sort. By the way, the fact that they could not produce the body proves that the Jews had not moved it. The Romans hadn't either – otherwise it could have been produced when the Christian Church began to prove a threat to the peace (which it did within a few weeks). This really only leaves the disciples as possible grave robbers. But the longer you think about the possibility the more incredible it appears. Even if they could have got through the guard that was posted on the tomb, I can't see that they would have been willing to be torn limb from limb for what they knew quite well was a fraud. You cannot possibly explain the sense of joy and confidence and power which radiates from the New Testament on the assumption that the early Christians were hypocrites, pretending Jesus was alive when they knew he was not. I do not know anyone who has studied the evidence who regards that as a possible explanation. Very well, then, if the body of Jesus was not removed by either his friends or his enemies,

that leaves only one possibility. It is that God raised him
from the dead, just as the amazed and triumphant Christians
claimed.

Consider the appearances of Jesus. He did not leave us with
an unexplained empty tomb. For forty days he appeared to his
disciples on a variety of occasions in a variety of locations. And
that disproves at once the view that these appearances might
have been hallucinations. You don't get the same hallucination
happening to lots of different people of different temperaments
in different places. On one occasion he appeared to over five
hundred people at once, most of whom were still alive to vouch
for it when Paul mentioned the fact in his first letter to the
Corinthians (1 Cor. 15: 6).

Consider the changed lives of his followers. 1 Cor. 15: 5–8
has a most interesting and very early list of those who met with
Jesus after his resurrection. The list originates within two or
three years of the event itself, and was already fixed in the
tradition before Paul became a Christian on the Damascus Road
in the mid-thirties A.D. It relates that Jesus rose from the dead
and appeared to Peter, then to the Twelve, then to five hundred
believers, then to James and last of all to Paul. Think of the
transformation that Resurrection brought about! Peter changed
from being a mercurial turncoat to a man of rock, on whose
courage and witness the early Church was founded. You can
hear the joy of the resurrection bursting out in his first letter
"Blessed be the God and Father of our Lord Jesus! By his great
mercy we have been born anew to a living hope through the
resurrection of Jesus Christ from the dead" (1 Peter 1: 3). The
Twelve, who had forsaken Jesus at his hour of need, now stand
up courageously for him in front of Jewish leaders, Roman
governors, and ordinary sceptical people in the streets. The five
hundred, who had presumably known Jesus in Galilee, are now
turned from a dispirited rabble into a humble, joyful, confident
Church. James, who along with Jesus' other brothers had been
very dubious about him while he was alive (what brothers
wouldn't?) now becomes a believer after it is all over. Why?
The New Testament tells us why: "He appeared to James" (1
Cor. 15: 7). So James turned from sceptical brother to cour-
ageous leader of the church in Jerusalem, eventually to suffer
martyrdom for the brother he had once laughed at. And Paul,
well, everyone knows about Paul. The greatest opponent of
Jesus was converted into the greatest disciple. Why? "Last of
all he appeared to me." When you consider honestly and

soberly the change in the lives of these men, and the way they all put it down to the resurrection, then I think you will agree that we have strong evidence that the resurrection did in fact take place.

The rise of the Church, the empty tomb, the resurrection appearances, the changed lives of his followers form our strands in a single rope. All the evidence indicates that Jesus did in fact rise from the dead. That is why his followers were convinced he was more than man. That is why they thought him worthy of worship. That is why they were so confident. That is why they spread so rapidly. And that is why millions of Christians all down the ages and all across the globe have been able to add their testimony to the fact that Jesus rose from the dead. *He lives, and they know it!*

All in all, this adds up to a very powerful reason why you should bother with Jesus. If he rose from the dead, he is the Son of God. If he rose from the dead, he is alive and you can have dealings with him. If he rose from the dead, he can guide you in this life and the next – the only person in the world qualified to do so. It would be well to bother about him while there is time.

Bother because he can change your life

THE EVIDENCE FOR the resurrection of Jesus does not end with the first century. Indeed, one of the most remarkable proofs of its truth is this. Unlike most historical events, which become more uncertain the further you are from them, the conviction that Jesus rose and is alive has grown down the centuries. Now you can meet not a Peter, a John, a Paul and perhaps five hundred Christians who could assure you that he is alive and in business, but millions all over the world. They can do so partly because of the historical evidence, but mainly because they know him. Not know about him, mind you: *know him*. There's a world of difference between the two.

When I know about someone he is just a flat, historical figure to me, whether he is alive today or whether he lived long ago. But he springs into 3-D the moment I get to know him. First we are introduced: then we spend time together: then we become friends: then we get to know one another at depth.

It is rather like that with Jesus. For years I knew about him in a flat, historical sort of way. And then one day I came to see that if he rose from the grave (which I vaguely believed) he was alive, available, and I could come to know him. So I asked him to make himself real to me. I asked him to become my friend, my intimate. I asked him to set to work changing me by his transforming friendship into what I ought to be. From that day onwards, and it is more than twenty years ago, I can honestly say that I do not just know about Jesus. I know him.

In one way, things haven't changed much since he walked this earth. Then he used to change men's lives as they came into close contact with him. Think of James and John, those "sons of thunder" as they were nicknamed, hot-tempered and blood-thirsty couple that they were. And then read the first letter of John and see the love of Christ simply flowing from it. You will appreciate what a genius Jesus was at changing character for the better.

Or look at Mary of Magdala, not only a prostitute but possessed by demons: she had been deep into the occult. Jesus changed her whole life. She became pure and loving, an absolutely devoted follower of his, and first witness of the resurrection. Or think of James and Jude, two of the brothers of Jesus, who did not think much of their famous brother while he was around, but came to discover who he was after the resurrection and both wrote letters in the New Testament declaring themselves his slaves!

That life-changing pattern continued once Jesus left this earth, and his Spirit came to live inside the hearts and lives of believers. The Spirit enabled Jesus to do in many lives what he could do, during his life time, only in the few that he met: transform them. Indeed, the whole purpose of the Spirit in the lives of Christians is to make them like Jesus. He gradually changes us into Christ's likeness as we live close to him (2 Cor. 3: 18 is a wonderful verse about this). The change in the early Christians is striking. They were not "nice, respectable folk, who enjoyed going to church on Sunday". They were "immoral, idolaters, adulterers, sexual perverts, thieves, greedy, drunkards, revilers, robbers". "Such were some of you," writes Paul (1 Cor. 6: 9f). "But you were washed, you were sanctified, you were justified in the name of the Lord Jesus and by the Spirit of our God." That is the supreme glory of Jesus: taking lives that have been spoiled by selfishness and sin, and transforming them so that they began to shine with light borrowed from his own character. That is what the Christian life is all about. The living, risen Jesus still changes lives.

Think of some of the well known people of our day. Stalin was one of the nastiest tyrants our generation has seen, dedicated to atheism and cruelty. His daughter Svetlana has discovered that Jesus is alive and real. He has changed Svetlana's life. Or think how another prominent Russian, Solzhenitzyn was enabled to sustain the fierce persecution to which he was subject in the Siberian labour camp; it was because Jesus Christ gave him ideals, courage and strength.

Cross the Atlantic, and what do you find? On the one hand the President of the U.S.A., Jimmy Carter, freely acknowledging that faith in Jesus has been the most life-changing factor in the whole of his career. On the other, Charles Colson, hatchet man of the White House during the Nixon Administration, rejoicing in the new life which Jesus has given him and dedicating his life to letting others know (be they politicians or prisoners), that Jesus Christ is alive and mighty to transform people today. At the other end of the American spectrum, the leading revolutionary and Black Power radical, Eldridge Cleaver has suddenly discovered that Jesus Christ is alive. He knows himself to be forgiven by Jesus. He knows Jesus' power to clean the hatred out of his life. He is already discovering that to follow Jesus is the most exciting cause any man can espouse. And he has returned voluntarily to the United States to face the music – if necessary a long jail sentence for his previous crimes.

Or come to England. Here you will find George Thomas, Speaker of the House of Commons, quietly living his life with Christ and for him, in an integrity of politics and character which wins respect from all. He found the living Christ in the valleys of his native Wales as a teenager, and has devoted his life serving his fellows in Jesus' name. You will find a pop star like Cliff Richard, turned round in mid-career by Jesus Christ, and now devoting much of his time to concerts for helping reach poverty-stricken people in the third world with food and the good news of Jesus. You will find an international footballer like Don Nardiello of Coventry City courageously following Jesus Christ in the highly competitive world of professional soccer. It shows in his speech and behaviour.

But it is not just the well-known people that Jesus is interested in. I think of a lovely chap I know, a labourer, who found Jesus when he was in prison. So did his wife while waiting for him to come out. You should just see the love and happiness in their married life now. Prison reminds me of another ex-con, a car thief, whom I know well. He found Christ while in Reading Gaol. Guess what he is doing now? He's a vicar!

I think of the scores and scores of agnostic students each year in Oxford where I work who come to find in Jesus Christ a living, challenging friend and guide. And you can always notice the difference he makes. A new joy, a new concern for other people, a new ability to break with bad habits, a new delight in prayer, a love of the company of other friends of Jesus, an unselfishness that was not there before. It does not matter what background people come from. I think at the moment of a cultured Japanese, a rich Moslem from Turkey, a gentle Hindu, a gangster in prison for life, a prostitute, many middle-class kids, a carpenter, an able Jew. Jesus has made room for all of them. He is the man for all seasons and the man for all types.

Because he is alive, you can talk to him – once you have been introduced. You can enjoy his company, and that makes such a difference to the loneliness which comes to all of us from time to time. "I am with you always" is his promise (Matt. 28: 20).

Because he is alive you can ask him for his help when the pressures are on and when temptation seems irresistible. "Greater is he who is in you than he who is in the world," says the Good Book. And it's true. You can prove it for yourself. Just say "Lord, help me" – and he will.

Because he is alive you can come back to him when you have done something you could kick yourself for. You can say "I've been a fool. So sorry." And "if we confess our sins he is faithful and just to forgive us our sins and cleanse us from all unrighteousness". (1 John 1: 9).

Because he is alive you can meet him in the lives of other Christians and recognise the changes he is making there, rejoice in them, and learn from them.

Because he is alive you can entrust your job, your marriage, your future to him. As Peter puts it with admirable simplicity: "Throw all your worries on him. For it matters to him about you." (1 Peter 5: 7).

Because he is alive even retirement and old age need not terrify you. You need never retire from his employment. He will not scrap you when you are grey-headed. And when one day you have to die, he will whisper to you, "Be of good cheer. It is I. Be not afraid."

Living with Jesus like this cannot fail to transform your life. And isn't that what you really want, at any rate in your better moments? Then what's all this about "Why bother with Jesus?" He is the very one you need if you are going to be the man or woman you could be – and were meant to be. Don't turn up the chance of a lifetime.

II

Bother because you need him

"I DON'T NEED Jesus Christ," do I hear you say? "He's just for weak characters who need a crutch in life." Really? Then let me ask you a question or two.

Do you know a lot of love in your life? Sex, sure. But lasting love? A love that puts up with you when you are being impossible? A love that makes your family a joy to enter? A love which grows as you and your Mrs. get older? A love that overflows to other people in a free, unjudging acceptance? If you haven't got a lot of that in your life, you need to bother about Jesus. For he can provide it.

Do you find yourself really fulfilled in life? Many folks think that happiness is the result of getting more and more money and possessions. Have you found that doesn't satisfy? Others think that if only you get fame or power or achieve your ambitions that will automatically make you happy. Have you discovered that isn't true either? Happiness is a state of mind. Happiness is more or less independent of your outward circumstances. St. Paul wrote, as he lay chained in prison, "Rejoice in the Lord always, and again I say, rejoice" (Phil. 4: 4). Could you do that if you were in prison? If not, you need the one who can bring joy like that. It is Jesus.

How about your relationships? Do you find that you actually do what you set out to do – treat all men as you would like them to treat you? Are you even-tempered, thoughtful, kind, giving people the benefit of the doubt? If you find that question hard to answer, ask your wife, your secretary, your workmates or school friends or business colleagues. We seem to be a lot better at relating to things than to people these days. People are so much more unpredictable! If the whole area of relationships is one where you are weak, you need to get acquainted with the expert in the subject, Jesus. He tells us that his new commandment for us is to love one another. He also tells us that he can provide the love within us. It is the first and choicest of the fruits produced by his Spirit once he is allowed to take root in us.

Or look at it another way. Do you not find *the whole question of the future* exceedingly perplexing? It makes no difference whether you are in a union or in management, a girl wondering whether to get married (and reckoning that one in three marriages pack up; will hers?) or a boy wondering what to do when he leaves school (and perhaps having to start off by joining the dole queue). On any showing, life is difficult, and decisions are harrowing. Is there not something to be said for having the personal guidance and care of the one who has been this way before us, and knows every snag, every problem? He holds the future in those hands of his. I do not promise you easy answers if you entrust yourself to him. In many ways problems get harder. But the joy of having someone who loves you completely to share them with is something I would not trade for a million pounds.

I wonder if you have any *weaknesses* that get you down time and again? Or are you a perfect sort of bloke, like William Weddell, Esq., whose imposing monument stands in Ripon Cathedral? "To the memory of William Weddell, Esq. of Newby, in whom every virtue that ennobles the human mind was united with every elegance that adorns it, this monument, a faint emblem of his refined taste, is dedicated by his widow." We laugh when we see something like that. We know that human beings are not like that. We aren't, ourselves: far from it. Do we not need the Master-carpenter of Nazareth to get to work on the rough wood of our lives and carve in us something of his own lovely character?

There are two other areas which are not often spoken about these days, and yet every man, woman and child on this earth needs them: *a forgiveness that wipes out the past, and a life that lasts into the future.* I have yet to know anyone who has not got a skeleton or two rattling around the hidden cupboards of his life. And the doctors, the psychiatrists, and the "snap-out-of-it" brigade cannot get rid of it for us. There are things we have done which we would give anything not to have done: there are guilty acts in our own lives, which we ourselves did *and meant to do,* but of which we are now deeply ashamed. We feel dirty as a result of them, and we do not know how we can get spring-cleaned. That is one of our basic needs. And there is an equal need as we live through our three score years and ten. Life seems endless when we are teenagers. It seems very short in our fifties. And by the time we are seventy-one, we realise we are living on borrowed time. Can this life be all there is? Deep down we feel it can't be. And yet how can we be sure about anything beyond it?

Jesus Christ is the only one who can meet these two most universal of all the needs of man. His death on the cross wiped out our sins. When he looks at the very things we feel we can never forget, and can never forgive ourselves for, he says "Your sins and your iniquities I will remember no more . . . Happy is the man whose transgressions are forgiven and whose sin is

covered ... There is no condemnation to the man who is in
Christ Jesus ... He has once suffered for sins, the just for the
unjust, that he might bring us to God." Where else do you get
an offer like that?

And the whole purpose of his coming to earth was to make
eternal life a possibility for us. Eternal life does not start when
you are dead. It starts before you are dead, or else it does not
start at all. "This is eternal life, to know the only true God and
Jesus Christ whom he has sent," said Jesus (John 17: 3). St.
John put it with great simplicity, "He who has the Son has life,
and he who does not have the Son does not have life" (1 John
5:12). Eternal life is not an added *quantity* of life, but a new
quality of life – such as a boy senses when he gets his first
motor-cycle, or a girl on her wedding day. A new dimension
to living seems to have opened up. That is how it is when Jesus
Christ comes into our lives. Eternal life begins then, and carries
on through death for ever, in the company of the Lord we love.

O.K. then, if you don't want eternal life and don't see the
need for forgiveness, I can understand you saying 'Why bother
with Jesus?" That is your decision. He will respect it. He never
forces himself on anybody – that is not love's way. But if, in
addition to the need for moral strength, deep satisfaction, a life
full of love, his guidance, and the ability to develop really
caring relationships with others, you are aware of these two
great needs of forgiveness and eternal life, I can tell you one
thing. Nobody will be able to give them to you but Jesus. If you
don't bother about him it will be pointless to bother about
them.

12

Bother because he calls you

THE IDEA HAS got around that to be a Christian is a soft option. Incredible! It just shows how good the Enemy's propaganda machine is. As a matter of fact, only the people with courage, the folks who are prepared to swim against the current, are to be found among the committed followers of Jesus Christ. They may be little old ladies, or tough business executives, navvies or newspaper men, but they all need moral courage if they are going to stand up and be counted among the friends of Jesus. He never offered us an easy time. He had a tough one, and he warned us that we would, too. We would have to love him better than father or mother or home or job. We would have to be unashamed of him in any company. We would have to be prepared to stick out as unmistakably as a city on a hill top. We would have to be in a minority. We would have to go the way of the cross in some form or other. It would not be easy to follow Jesus. It never has been and it isn't today.

So let's get out of our heads for good and all the "Come to Jesus and everything in the garden will be lovely" sort of approach. If you have ever heard preachers talk like that, forget them. That is not the authentic article, but a sugary imitation of genuine Christianity.

Listen to the first recorded words of Jesus. "Jesus came into Galilee, preaching the gospel of God, and saying, 'The time is fulfilled, and the kingdom of God is at hand. Repent, and believe in the gospel.' And passing along by the Sea of Galilee, he saw Simon and Andrew his brother casting a net into the sea; for they were fishermen. And Jesus said to them, 'Follow me, and I will make you to become fishers of men.' And immediately they left their nets and followed him. And going on a little farther, he saw James the son of Zebedee, and John his brother, who were in their boat, mending the nets. Immediately he called them; and they left their father Zebedee in the boat with the hired servants, and followed him" (Mark 1: 15–20).

There are lots of interesting things in that short story. Notice how Jesus strides onto the scene and takes these tough fishermen by storm. They would not follow just anybody! He must have convinced them that he did indeed bring God's Kingdom in his own person. They must have seen him as "good news" – for that is what "gospel" means. Do you think of Jesus that way? And the Jesus who brings good news of all that God's kingly rule can mean in a man's life tells them that time is up. They need to decide for him or against him. Are they going to repent, and change their self-centred attitude or not? Are they going to trust him, or not? Will they or will they not launch out on a life following him, entrusting themselves to his sure hands for all that the future may bring? Will they rate him higher than their job, higher even than their family and their workmates?

Such was the challenge then. We all know what they did about it. But the challenge still comes to us now. Jesus says to you, who have got this far in the book, "The time is fulfilled." Time is up. You have hung around long enough. You may only know a little about him, but you know enough to entrust yourself. It is a matter of the will. How about it?

"But what am I supposed to do?" you may ask. Nothing very complicated: just something very tough. He says, "Repent." That means, have done with all you know to be wrong. It doesn't mean you have to give it up before you enlist in his cause: you can't. That's what you need a Saviour for. But it does mean you must be willing for him to cut out all the diseased parts of your life. He is the skilled surgeon. You can trust him not to hurt you more than is necessary, and only to remove what is hopelessly diseased. You don't have to rustle up lots of crocodile tears about how wicked you are. You simply have to let go and let God. Say to him, "Jesus, come and clean me up. I really want it, whatever it costs."

Surely that is hard enough? No, there is more to come. Nobody said it was going to be an easy ride. From now on it is the kingdom of God that is going to control your life, remember? Very well, the King has got to come first. Before those "nets" of yours: all the things your life is taken up with. Before the "boats": all the possessions that seem so important. Before the "hired servants": all the folk who might laugh at you. Before "Zebedee": all those nearest and dearest to you who might not like the change of direction. Are you willing to put him first? If not, keep clear of Jesus. He is not the man for you. He is looking for revolutionary characters who will pledge their all in his cause. He gave his all for us . . .

"O.K.," you say "I am prepared. At least, I think I am." Fine. Then the next step is simple, but it is very difficult. Simple because a child can do it. Difficult because it takes the humility of a child to get round to doing it. Jesus says "Believe in the good news." Do you feel you believe in it already? Wait a moment. The good news is first and foremost bad news: it tells us that without Jesus we are hopelessly lost. Do you admit that? Do you recognise that your good deeds are not enough to win God's favour? That you can't earn it by going to church or giving your money to the poor? You enter the Kingdom through a very narrow door. That door is near a cross. And on that cross hangs one with a filthy burden on his back. As you look, you see to your horror that the burden is made up of all the wrong things, wrong thoughts, wrong attitudes, wrong words, wrong habits of which you are guilty. He looks straight at you, as he hangs there, and says, "Do you believe in the good news? I hang there for you. I bear your burdens so that you may never be choked by them. Will you accept a free pardon – because I have taken your place?" To say "Yes, Lord: thank you so much" is very simple, but incredibly humbling. Nobody has ever yet entered the Kingdom any other way. No exceptions will be made for you. You come on your knees, you come crying for pardon, you come with tears of gratitude in your eyes, if you "believe in the gospel". Do you? If so, just kneel down now, wherever you are, and thank the Lord for what he has done to make you accepted. Entrust your whole life to him

in glad response. Remember, it is for keeps. He will not abuse
your trust.

What next? These moments pass, do they not? What about
that future – spent with Christ? Well, the first disciples had to
learn an important fact. They were disciples: that word means
"learners". They put their "L" plates up. And so must you. As
a matter of fact, you keep them up for the rest of your earthly
life. You will never "pass your test" and become independent
of your Instructor. He will sit alongside you in the front of your
car for the rest of life's journey now that you have let him in.
He knows the perils and the problems of the route. He is
infinitely experienced. He says, "Follow me." How do I do
that? Two ways spring to mind at once.

First, *find out his instructions*. There is a perfectly adequate
manual in the front of the car. The Scriptures show you all you
need to know about the journey, and give you his instructions
on how to finish it successfully. Read that manual. There are
modern translations of it, like the "Good News Bible". There
are Bible-reading helps like the Scripture Union. But if you
want to follow his instructions you simply must, yes *must*,
study that driving manual.

The other thing, of course, which those first disciples realised is that *you do not follow him alone*. It is a "together"
thing. They were called together. They followed together.
They came to love and trust each other, because they had Jesus
as their common Instructor. You need Christian people if you
are to follow Jesus properly. Go and find some. Tell them that
you have joined the gang. And ask them to help you on your
way. Public worship is a "must". So is some informal gathering
with one person or a group of people with whom you can let
your hair down and voice your hesitations, problems and hang-
ups. You're going to need something like that, especially in the
early days. Go looking for it straight away.

Jesus has the same purpose in store for us as he had for these
first followers. "I will make you become fishers of men." We are
far from that when we come to him all raw and fresh. He has a
lot of work to do on us as we put up our "L" plates and begin to
follow him. But his intention is that we shall bring other people
to bother about him, and know him and love him. His strategy
is to work through people like us to win people like us. Simple,
isn't it? And effective. If we let him, that is. Some folks say "I
couldn't possibly talk about religion to my friends." You aren't
being asked to, silly. Religion is bad news. Jesus is good news.

Tell them what you are beginning to discover in your Friend
and Lord, Jesus. And since it is to be a lifelong occupation, the
sooner you start the better. Go and tell someone today if you
have entrusted your life to Christ. You don't necessarily need to
pick the biggest tough in your circle of friends. But you do need
to open your lips right away. Secret disciples are no use to
Jesus. They never achieved much in the fishing business. Jesus
depends on your recommendation among your friends. And
there's another side to it: typical of him. When you pluck up
courage to speak about him, however falteringly, he gives you
a great sense of assurance that you do belong to him, and that
his Holy Spirit is at work in you. That's the point of Romans
10: 9, 10 and Mark 13: 11. They are good verses. Look them
up!

Are you still wondering whether to take the plunge? Then let
me remind you of one striking thing about this little passage in
Mark, chapter one. Jesus did not say "Just you follow me and
you will have a marvellous time." Jesus did not say "Just you
follow me and I will give you lots of desirable things." Jesus
did not wheedle them and say "Please, please, come and follow
me." He commanded them to do it. No nonsense about it. He
had already, we must believe, shown them who he was, and
what he could do for them. He has certainly not left *us* in doubt
on these things. Now he says, in effect, "Get on with it. Decide.
Not because of what you will get out of it. Not because you will
have an easier time: you won't. Not because I plead with you
(although I do). But come and follow me because that is the
only possible right response to my love which has gone to such
lengths for you. Come and follow me because there is no other
way you can find life and bring it to others. I do not merely
advise you. I do not cajole you. I, your Lord and your God am
willing to be your Saviour and your Friend. I command you. I
tell you. Come, follow me."

Will you?

13

Get big by bothering

A celebrated London employment agency makes the proud boast that it got big by bothering. There is a lot in that. Growth does not happen by accident in business: nor does it in the Christian life. You only get big by bothering.

Now the New Testament certainly expects us to get big. But one part of us that should not grow is our head! You will not need a larger size in hats the longer you go on with Christ. Quite the reverse. The more time you spend in his company the more you will see yourself in your true colours, and the more you will realise that any progress is to be credited to him not you. (Simon Peter knew that from painful personal experience. The man who had thought he could never fall away from Jesus denied him three times the night when Jesus was arrested. He writes later, with feeling, "Clothe yourselves, all of you, with humility toward one another, for 'God opposes the proud, but gives grace to the humble.' Humble yourselves therefore under the mighty hand of God so that in due time he may exalt you" (1 Peter 5:5f).) No, the areas in which we grow big are quite different.

Grow big by eating. However old you are when you come to faith, you then become a spiritual babe. Just as the baby longs for its bottle, so the new Christian will long for "the pure spiritual milk, that by it he may grow up" (1 Peter 2: 2). Spiritual milk includes Bible reading, and it helps no end to get some system like the Scripture Union (from a local Christian bookshop or 5 Wigmore Street, London W.1) and to find some Christian friend who can read it with you a bit and give you a hand. But spiritual food is wider than Bible reading. It includes prayer -- and here again we shall need help. It includes the Holy Communion: Jesus left us a meal to remember him by, and we need it regularly. In it we not only remember that we owe everything to his body and his blood shed for us: we feast with the risen Lord, and we look forward to being with him when this life is over.

Grow big by trusting. "We are bound to give thanks to God always, for you brothers, because your trust is growing all the time" (2 Thess. 1: 3). The new believers in this Northern Greek City were learning to trust the Lord whom they could not see. They trusted him to build them up in love for other Christians, to teach them, and to see them through hard times. They trusted him with their problems and their need for guidance. And this is how they grew in confidence and in experience of the Lord. "Commit your way unto the Lord. Trust also in him. And he will act" said the Old Testament (Psalm 37: 5). The Thessalonians began falteringly to exercise this trust: and so can you. It is a great way to grow.

Grow big by sharing. Christianity is not a solo trip. It has to be done in a team. The Boss is not interested in changing individuals alone. He wants to show what he can do in a people who trust him. The New Testament puts this point in various ways. Here are a couple out of the same letter, written to Christians in what was then the capital city of modern Turkey, Ephesus. You folks, says the apostle, are like limbs in a body. You need to grow and to keep pace in your growth with one another, so that the whole body is co-ordinated. "Speaking the truth in love we are to grow up in every way into him who is the head, into Christ. From him the whole body, joined and knit together by every ligament, makes bodily growth when every part is working properly, and builds itself up in love" (Eph. 4:15ff). Isn't that a marvellous picture of our need for a close, supportive Christian fellowship? He put it in a different way in chapter 2:21. Christians are not limbs in a body this time but stones in a building. And as he watches he seems to see "the whole structure joined together and growing into a holy temple for the Lord. You, too, are built into this temple and together become a place where the Holy Spirit lives." How about that for privilege? Doesn't it put a new perspective on our mutual relationships as Christians? We grow by being together. It can't be done on our own.

Get big by growing fruit. In Colossians 1:10 Paul longs that the Colossians may lead a life worthy of the Lord, learn to please him in everything they do, and bear fruit in every good work while they increase in the knowledge of God. Fruit bearing is the natural outcome of growth, and so it is when the Holy Spirit is planted in the soil of our lives. "Fruit" is used in the New Testament mainly to indicate change in our character and the conversion of other people to faith in Jesus: these are the qualities God longs to see in his followers who are growing.

None of these sides of growth happens by accident. You have to actually get a Bible out, you have to go to church, you have to start praying if you mean to grow big by eating. You have to commit problems and temptations to the Lord, if you want to grow big in faith. You have to get stuck in with other Christians if you are to grow up into one body, one building. If you are going to bear fruit, you have to ask the Holy Spirit to transform your character; and to take your courage in both hands and open your mouth to speak. These things require attention. But then growth always does. You get big by bothering. Don't be a dwarf Christian, will you?

You only get big by bothering . . .